Why Did the Government Need More Land?

The Louisiana Purchase
US History Books
Children's American History

BABY PROFESSOR
EDUCATION KIDS

Speedy Publishing LLC

40 E. Main St. #1156

Newark, DE 19711

www.speedypublishing.com

Copyright 2017

Thomas Jefferson

THE HISTORY BEHIND THE LOUISIANA PURCHASE

From 1699 to 1762, France had controlled the huge stretches of land to the west of the Mississippi. It was known as Louisiana. In 1762, France gave the land to Spain, which was then its ally against Britain. Napoleon took Louisiana back under French rule in the year 1800.

In order to plant more crops and support livestock for food, settlers had been moving to the west of the Appalachian Mountains as well as to the region that was known as the Northwest territory. As these areas became more crowded, it seemed logical to obtain more land to the west.

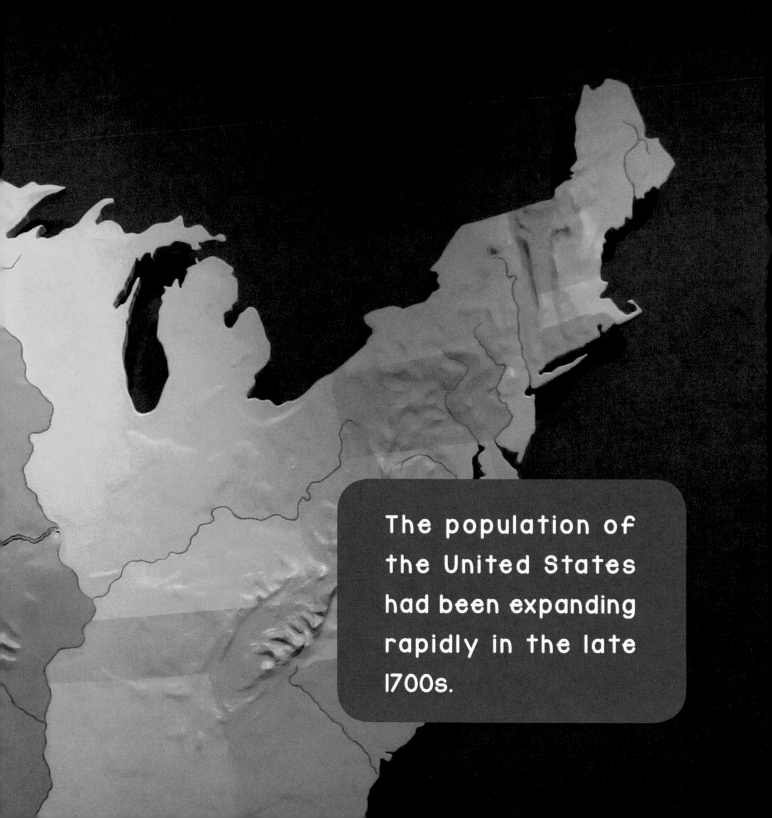

The population of the United States had been expanding rapidly in the late 1700s.

In this book, we're going to cover the Louisiana Purchase and why it was important to the United States. So, let's get right to it!

HOW MUCH DID IT COST?

The third president of the United States, Thomas Jefferson, wanted to purchase the seaport of New Orleans from the country of France. Because the mighty Mississippi River could be accessed through New Orleans, it was vital to businesses in the US.

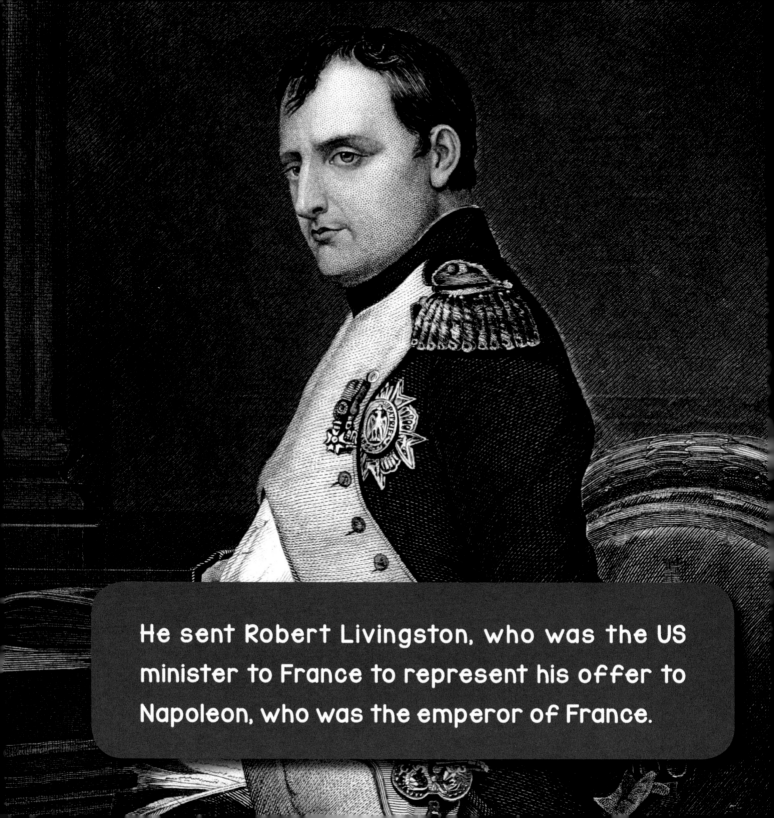

He sent Robert Livingston, who was the US minister to France to represent his offer to Napoleon, who was the emperor of France.

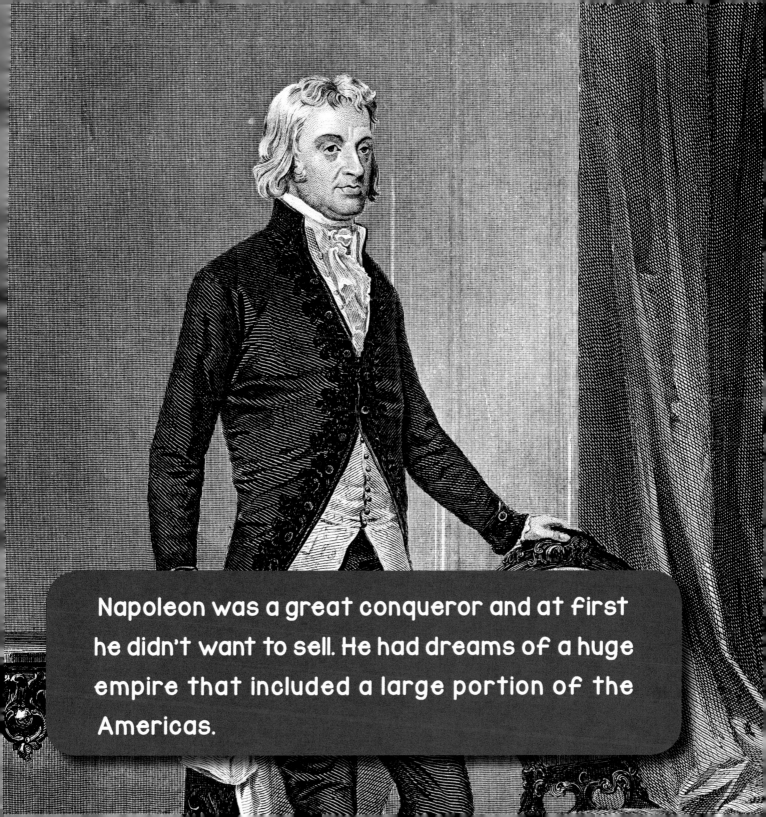

Napoleon was a great conqueror and at first he didn't want to sell. He had dreams of a huge empire that included a large portion of the Americas.

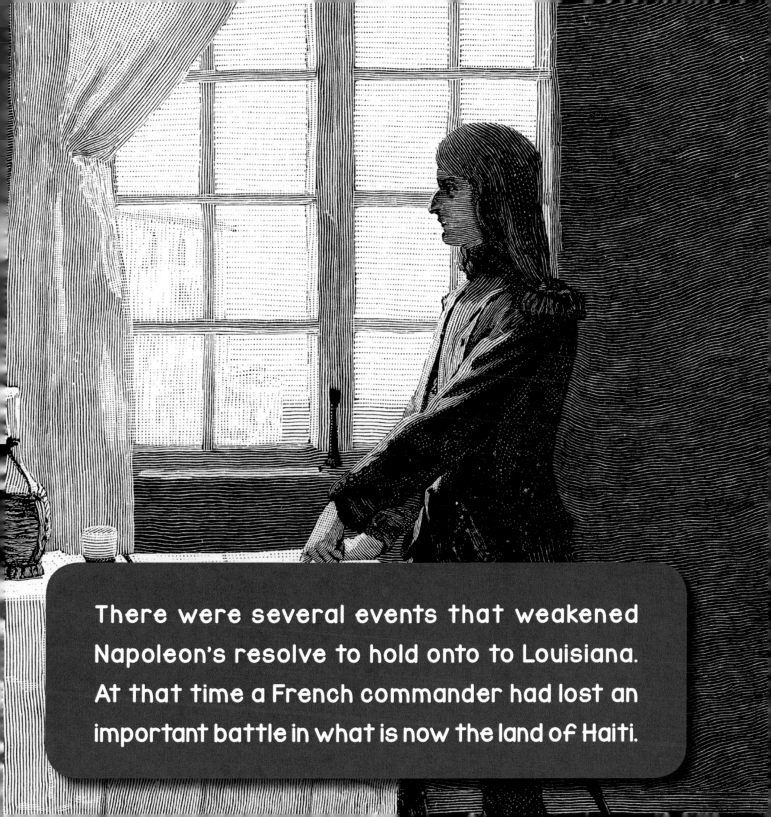

There were several events that weakened Napoleon's resolve to hold onto to Louisiana. At that time a French commander had lost an important battle in what is now the land of Haiti.

Ports on the southern coast of North America were now not accessible to the French because of this loss.

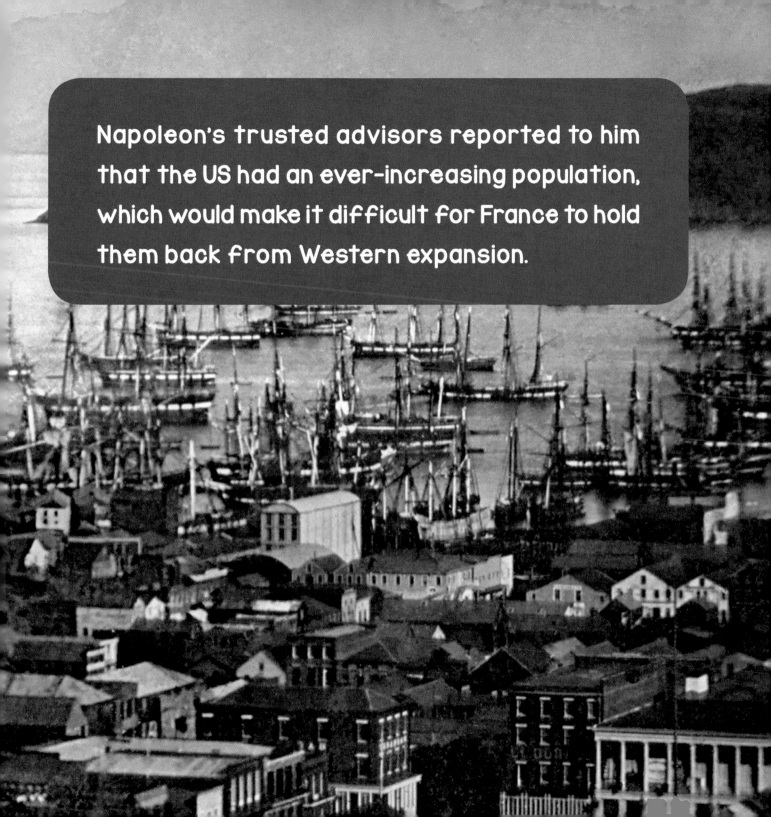

Napoleon's trusted advisors reported to him that the US had an ever-increasing population, which would make it difficult for France to hold them back from Western expansion.

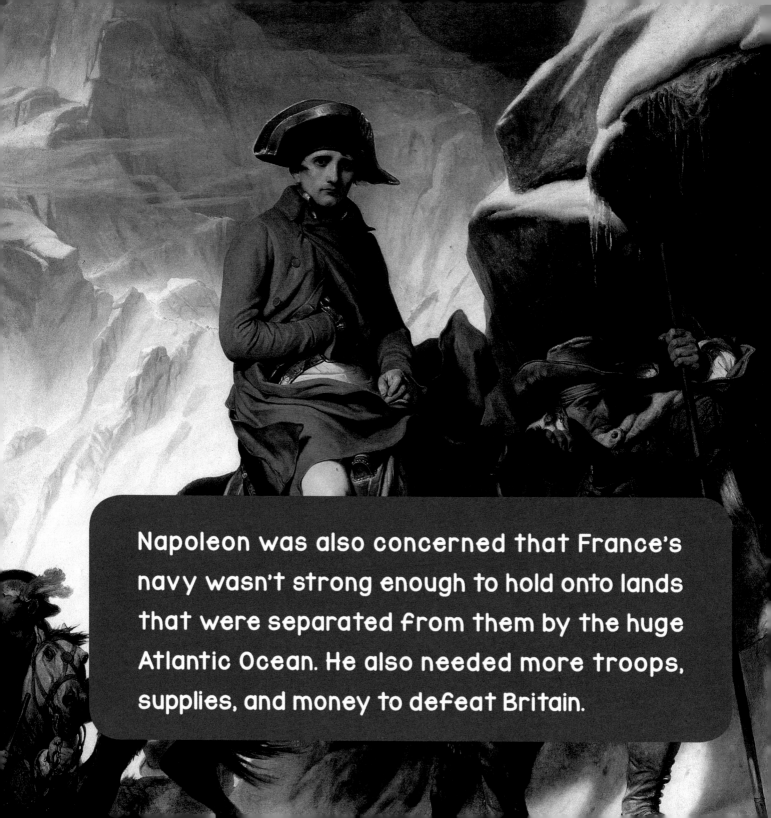

Napoleon was also concerned that France's navy wasn't strong enough to hold onto lands that were separated from them by the huge Atlantic Ocean. He also needed more troops, supplies, and money to defeat Britain.

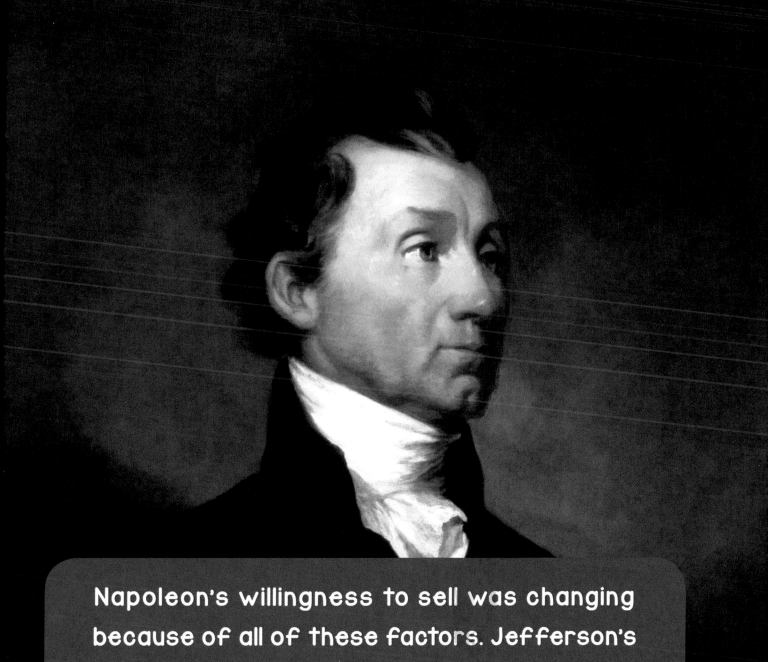

Napoleon's willingness to sell was changing because of all of these factors. Jefferson's timing was good. He enlisted James Monroe as a second envoy.

James Monroe was one of the Founding Fathers and would later become a US President. Monroe left for France and met up with Livingston so they could work together to negotiate the deal.

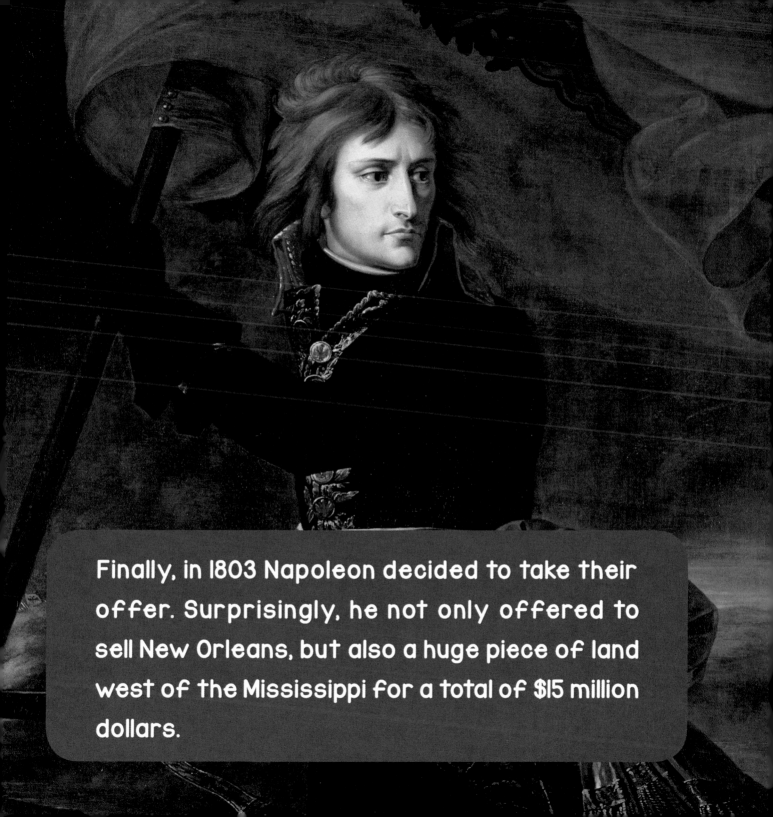

Finally, in 1803 Napoleon decided to take their offer. Surprisingly, he not only offered to sell New Orleans, but also a huge piece of land west of the Mississippi for a total of $15 million dollars.

HOW MUCH LAND WAS INCLUDED IN THE LOUISIANA PURCHASE?

The amount of land that Napoleon sold to Jefferson was huge. It was a total of 828,000 square miles.

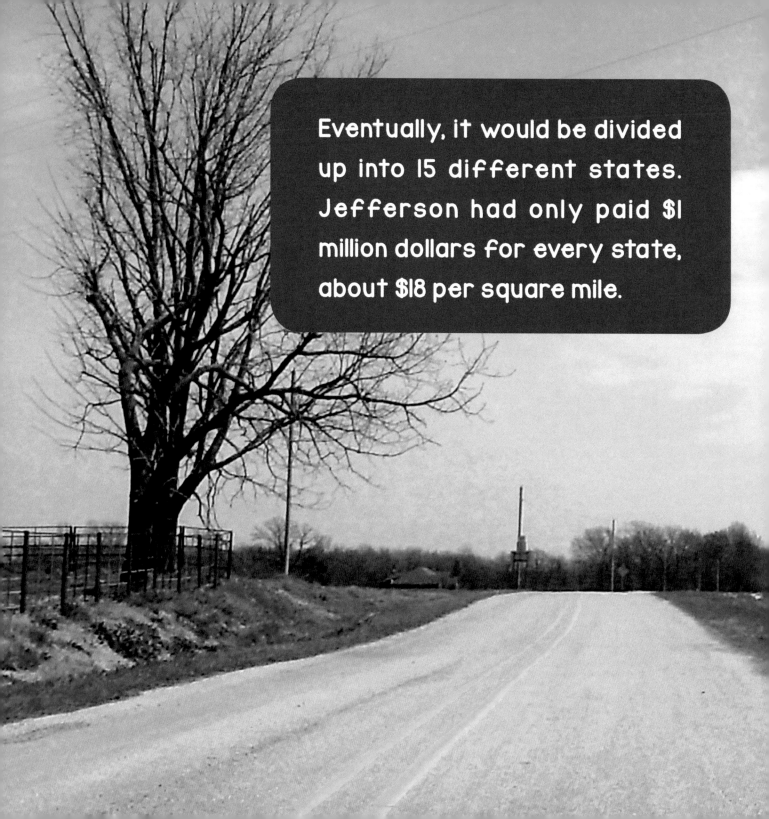

Eventually, it would be divided up into 15 different states. Jefferson had only paid $1 million dollars for every state, about $18 per square mile.

Since there are 640 acres in a square mile, this was about 3 cents an acre. The Louisiana Purchase was an amazing bargain!

The United States doubled in size overnight making it much more important among the world's nations. It was the beginnings of the US becoming a world power.

ALBERTA

SASKATCHEWAN

NA

NORTH DAKOTA

SOUTH DAKOTA

WYOMING

NEBRASK

Denver

COLORADO

KANS

NEW MEXICO

OKLA

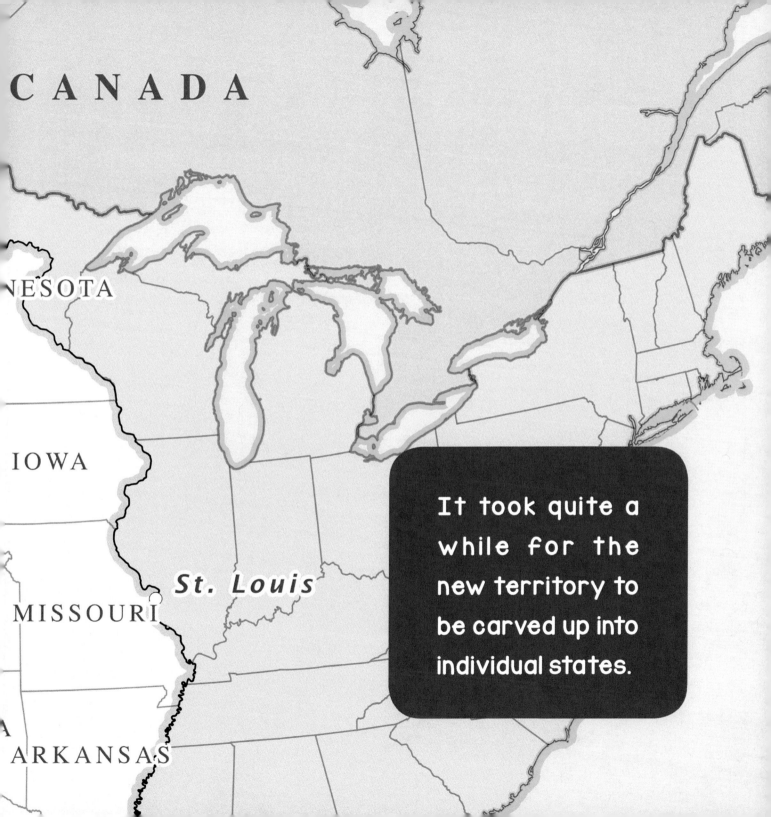

CANADA

NESOTA

IOWA

St. Louis

MISSOURI

ARKANSAS

It took quite a while for the new territory to be carved up into individual states.

OPPOSITION TO THE LOUISIANA PURCHASE

At the time that the deal for the Louisiana Purchase was struck, many US leaders were against the purchase. They were concerned that Jefferson didn't have the authority to make such an expensive purchase. They weren't even sure if Napoleon had the right to sell it. They were also concerned that Spain might wage war over the land since they were in possession of it before.

Congress almost cancelled the purchase and it passed by a very narrow vote 59 for the purchase to 57 opposed.

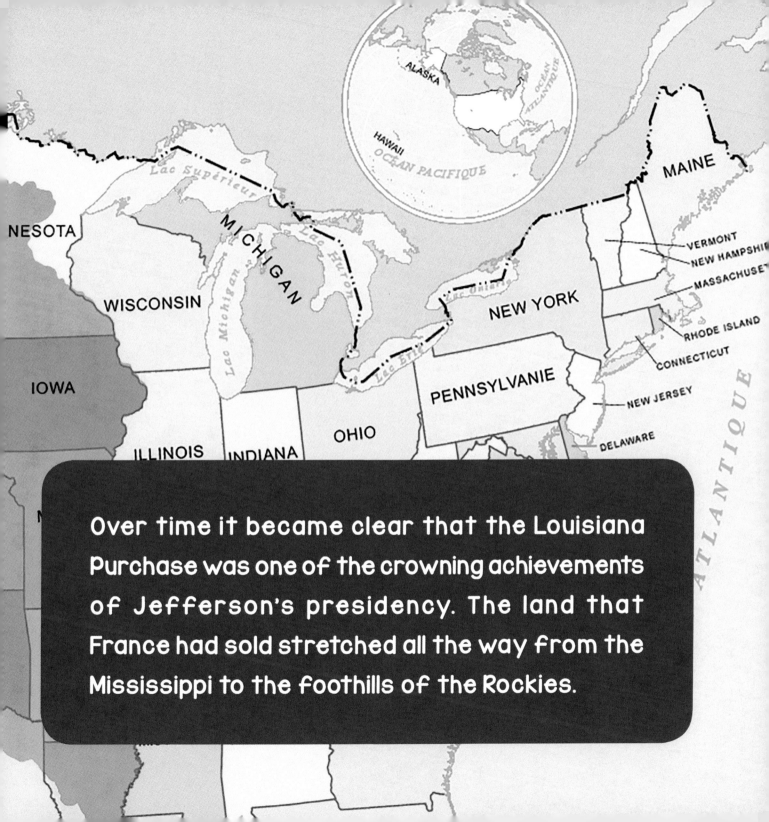

Over time it became clear that the Louisiana Purchase was one of the crowning achievements of Jefferson's presidency. The land that France had sold stretched all the way from the Mississippi to the foothills of the Rockies.

The fertile soils and other vital natural resources that the land contained weren't fully known by the France since the area was so large and unexplored at that time.

LEWIS AND CLARK

Much of the land in the Louisiana Purchase wasn't yet settled. Jefferson hired explorers to travel to the new lands and report back on their findings. The most famous of these expeditions was the one traveled by Captain Meriwether Lewis, who was Jefferson's private secretary, and his good friend Lieutenant William Clark.

Captain Meriwether Lewis and
Lieutenant William Clark

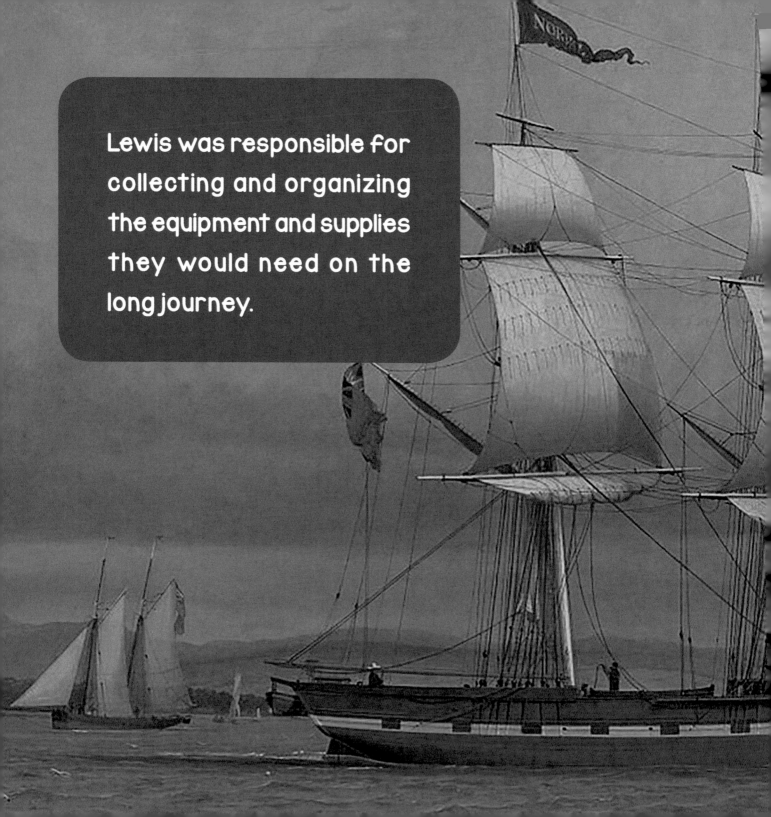

Lewis was responsible for collecting and organizing the equipment and supplies they would need on the long journey.

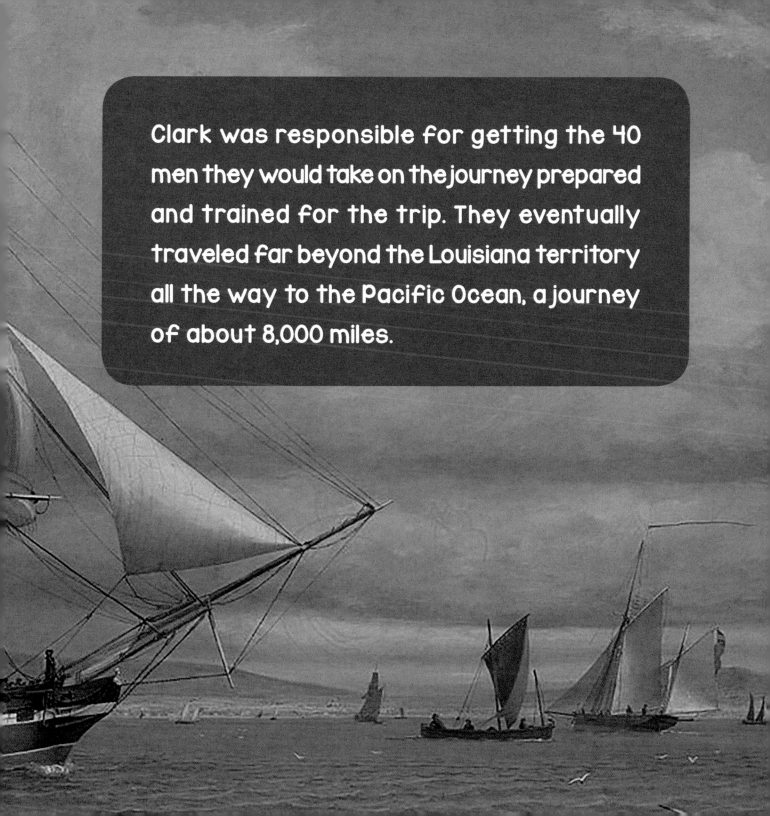

Clark was responsible for getting the 40 men they would take on the journey prepared and trained for the trip. They eventually traveled far beyond the Louisiana territory all the way to the Pacific Ocean, a journey of about 8,000 miles.

They left from the city of St. Louis, Missouri and came back to the same location from where they had departed two years later in 1806.

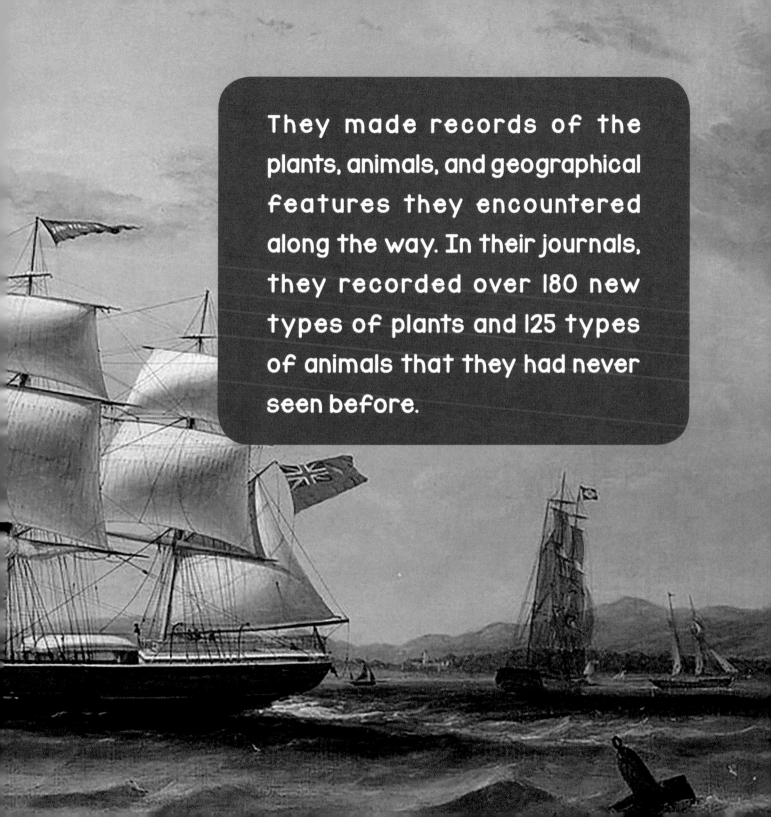

They made records of the plants, animals, and geographical features they encountered along the way. In their journals, they recorded over 180 new types of plants and 125 types of animals that they had never seen before.

Two birds were named after them, a woodpecker after Lewis and a nutcracker after Clark.

Woodpecker

Nutcracker

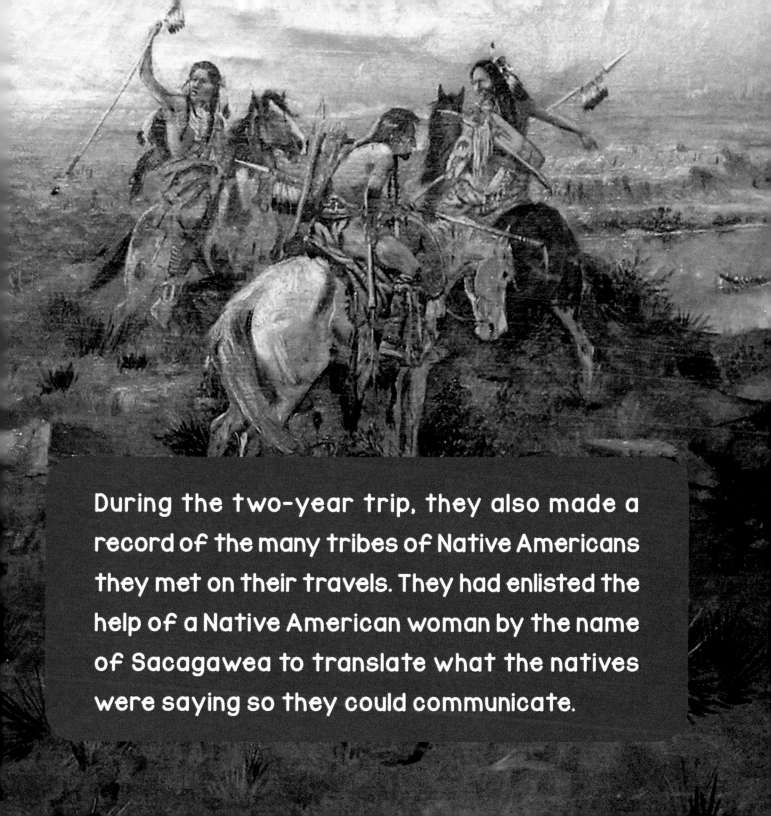

During the two-year trip, they also made a record of the many tribes of Native Americans they met on their travels. They had enlisted the help of a Native American woman by the name of Sacagawea to translate what the natives were saying so they could communicate.

One fateful day in May of 1805 as her husband, a French trapper by the name of Toussaint Charbonneau, was steering their boat on the Missouri River, they almost turned over. Charbonneau couldn't swim and while the other members of the party in the boat with them tried to paddle to shore, Sacagawea reached into the violent waves to grab their instruments and vital papers.

If it were not for her, we probably wouldn't know much about the expedition today. The Lewis and Clark Expedition eventually led to the United States acquisition of the Oregon Territory, which further expanded the United States. The Lewis and Clark Expedition wasn't the only expedition that Jefferson sent out. Another journey commissioned by Jefferson was the exploration of the Great Plains.

Pike's Peak, Colorado

The brigadier general Zebulon Montgomery Pike led this expedition and Pike's Peak in Colorado was named after him.

Another important expedition was the Red River Expedition. This team set out in 1806 to explore the Southwest. Jefferson chose astronomer and surveyor Thomas Freeman and Peter Custis, a naturalist, as leaders. Captain Richard Sparks was also commissioned to command the soldiers in the group. Unfortunately, they didn't fully achieve their goals for the journey since the Spanish confronted them in what is now northeastern Texas and they were forced to turn back.

WHY WAS THE LOUISIANA PURCHASE SO IMPORTANT?

The Journey Begins H

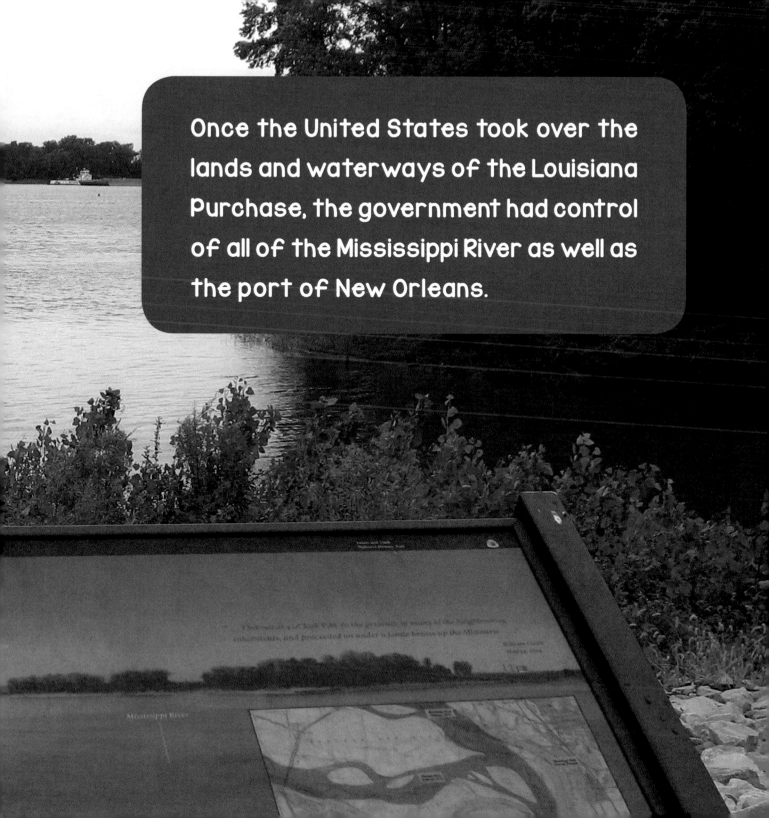

Once the United States took over the lands and waterways of the Louisiana Purchase, the government had control of all of the Mississippi River as well as the port of New Orleans.

This valuable waterway was used to transport crops and get farmers payment for their goods.

The land and natural resources including gold, silver, and other valuable ores of the Louisiana Purchase were worth thousands, perhaps millions of times more than the price that the United States had paid. With the expansion of this new territory, it was only a question of time before the United States acquired the land that would give it a continuous landmass from east coast to west coast. An added benefit of the purchase is that it eliminated the French presence in the continental US thereby increasing the security of the new nation.

Louisiana Purchase
1803 Bicentennial 2003
The Largest Real Estate Deal in History

SOLD $ 15 Million

Shreveport
Monroe
Rayville
Natchitoches
Alexandria
Lake Charles
Lafayette
Baton Rouge
New Orleans

Arkansas	Wyoming
Iowa	Minnesota
Missouri	Oklahoma
North Dakota	Colorado
South Dakota	Montana
Nebraska	Kansas
Louisiana	

Framers & Landscapers
Huey Franks   Matt Doughty
Dennis Odom   Wayne Chapman

Volunteer Painters
Ray Dry   Bob Townsend   Sara Ella Aycock
Gail Greer   Sue Whitman   Jane Upton Puderer
Cindy Odom   Maggie Yancey   Juanita Cochran
Donald Dees   Erin Yancey   Marcella Tatum

A SUMMARY OF THE LEGACY OF THE LOUISIANA PURCHASE

- ⇗ The purchase doubled the size of the US at a time when the nation was growing by leaps and bounds.

- ⇗ It ended the period of French Colonialism as well as reduced Spain's hold on lands in the US.

- ⇗ The US now had control over the important seaport of New Orleans and the access from there to the Mississippi River.

- ⇗ The massive forests and lands contributed to the lumber industry, farming, and the overall economy of the US.

- ⇗ The purchase was the beginning of other Western Expansion opportunities.

Awesome! Now you know more about why the Louisiana Purchase was important in American History. You can find more American History books from Baby Professor by searching the website of your favorite book retailer.

Visit

BABY PROFESSOR
EDUCATION KIDS

www.BabyProfessorBooks.com

to download Free Baby Professor eBooks
and view our catalog of new and exciting
Children's Books

Made in the USA
Monee, IL
03 August 2020